The
Attractive
Church

by

Kenneth White

GROVE BOOKS

BRAMCOTE   NOTTS.

CONTENTS

		Page
1.	Thirty Years of Change	3
2.	The Lingering Legacy	5
3.	The Language of Liturgy	6
4.	The Music of Liturgy	7
5.	The Gathering Church	8
6.	Awe in the Mind of the Believer	9
7.	Awe in the Eye of the Beholder	10
8.	The All-In Church	12
9.	The All-Out Church	14
10.	Motives for Change	16
11.	Motives for No Change	18
12.	The Wheels in Motion	20
13.	The Holiness of Beauty	22
	Appendix	23

THE ATTRACTIVE CHURCH

Some people like drinking and go to the pub; some like plays and go to the theatre; some like religion and go to church.

Going to church. We say it; we act it; we think it. We are known as good Christians because we *go to church*.

Never mind whether our non-church neighbours regard themselves as Christians ('I'm not a Jew or a Moslem, so I must be a Christian'); we carry the label of churchgoer and this ought to make us objects of interest. Of course, the chimpanzees' tea party makes *them* objects of interest, even amusement . . .

Going to church is a religious concept and a therapeutic activity. It suggests a certain attitude towards God whereby morally-inclined persons wend themselves to an unusual building at a regular time one day a week.

What happens when they get there ? Thirty years ago, a stock answer could be given. Not so now.

First Impression October 1979

ISSN 0305 3067

ISBN 0 905422 65 1

1. THIRTY YEARS OF CHANGE

'Peace if possible, but truth at any rate'

Martin Luther

The Thirty Years War (1618-48) in Germany between Catholics and Protestants was fought with firearms and polemics; the ammunition was gunpowder and doctrine. Both were explosive.

The past thirty years in the Church of England has seen a struggle; mercifully there has been no gunpowder but doctrine has charged not a few broadsides. To the churchgoer the effect has been experienced in the liturgy. Forms of service undreamt of thirty years ago are now commonplace and this is parallelled by multiple versions of Scripture.

It is worth dwelling upon these changes which have invaded the Church of England, especially as their effect varies. Let us say straight away that the degree of local change is influenced by the predilection of the minister. Despite Synodical Government the Church of England is still a clergy-dominated corpus. Yet it is not priest-ridden, as in some former times. The fact remains that the clergy are the professionals, the rest amateurs.

Until recently, one could attend any church and find a tolerably familiar service, give or take a few actions, garments and supplementary ejaculations in the Communion service. The format was 1662, with 1928 remaining a non-event. Then came Parish Communion.

At that time the church building was devoted exclusively to divine worship —and on Sundays only, that day still being widely observed as a day of non-work. People *went to church* and whether they realised it or not, their attitude to the building and its function was Victorian.

> The layout of most churches was: Nave and side aisle(s) with seating for congregation.

> Chancel for clergy and robed choir.

> Sanctuary (behind rails) for dispensing the bread and wine.

We are all familiar with the siting of the font, pulpit, lectern, organ and so forth; the standard Victorian arrangement.

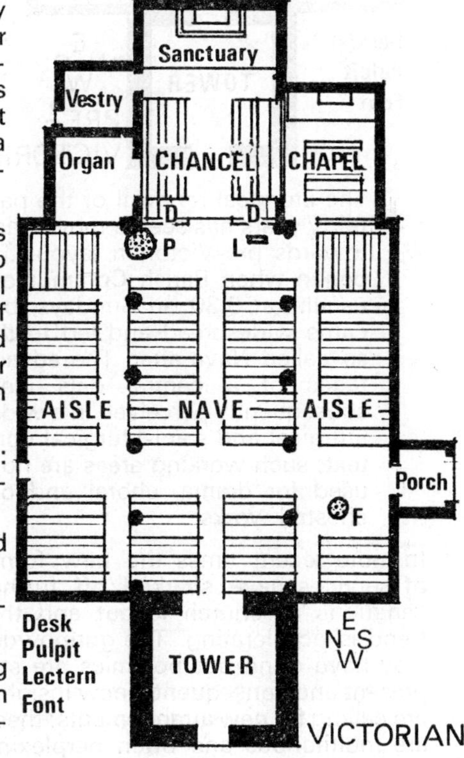

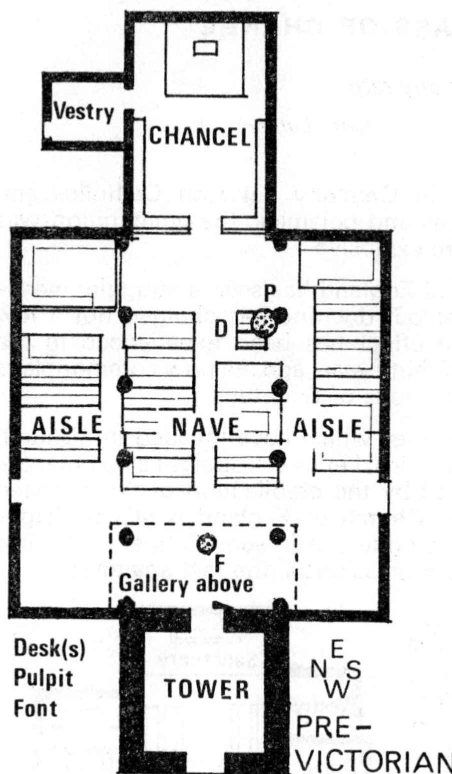

Prior to 1840 the layout which had developed through uniform use of reformed liturgy in the Prayer Book might have been:

Nave and side aisle(s) with seating for congregation and desks for clergy; choir (un-robed) and musicians in gallery or adjacent to con-gregation.

Chancel for communicants.

The pulpit would have dom-inated the church (unless the chancel screen was particu-larly massive) and the holy table would have been sub-ordinated; it was the Vic-torians who elevated it to the prime focus.

The liturgical renewal of the past thirty years has seen a move back towards pre-Victorian layouts. It began when Parish Communion, usually at 9.30 on Sundays, be-came widespread and led to the so-called Nave altar. The advan-tages of a central dais were subsequently perceived in a wider liturgical and semi-liturgical con-text; such working areas are now used for drama, choral and or-chestral works.

In more recent times the new forms of services have sparked off further variations of church layout and this trend is accelerating. The gunpowder may have gone but polemics are still present and consequently new insights are calling for new arrangements; these are multifarious and often perplexing to the flock.

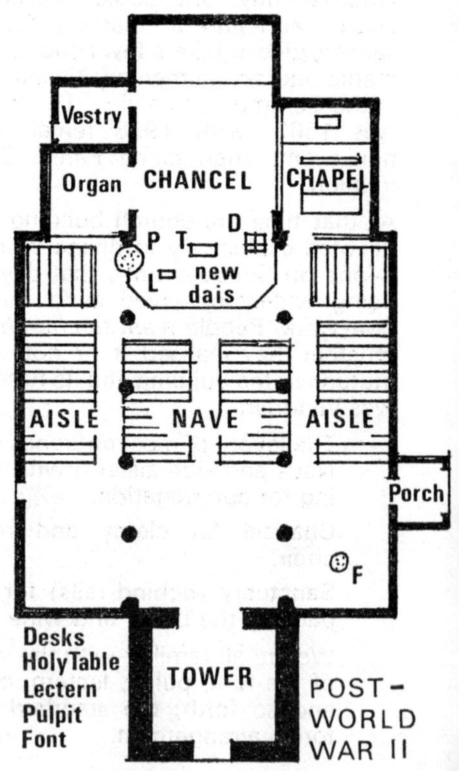

2. THE LINGERING LEGACY

'I don't like Series III because I've never tried it'

Although new modes of liturgy have come with a rush, they have not always received enthusiastic acceptance by PCCs and congregations. Most changes in church life are viewed with suspicion, and never more than in procedures for 'worship'. New words drive out long-recited familiar phrases, however imperfectly understood. Moreover, these new services are not always the official New Series, but also privately published Family Services, Hymn books, Praise books and local compilations. Charismatic overtones add further vocabulary.

The visitor may therefore no longer find the familiar set service but may be at a loss when confronted with a handful of booklets, most of which are used only in part. Clergy and readers have become selective and venturesome. This has produced hybrid forms of service, each man tending to say what is right in his own ears.

The impact upon the congregation varies and is subjective. To some members the liberty is exhilarating; to others, unsettling and distressing. There is nostalgia over lost 'majestic language' and letters like this are written to the press:

The changing church

SIR—If the Church of England is in urgent need of money, might the authorities not find it salutory to reflect on the number of older members whom they are alienating?

Many are being driven away from the Church, along with their contributions to the collections, by the alterations to be observed in many parishes such as the disappearance of Mattins, unfamiliar services, modern translations of the Bible and changes in the customary times of services.

D———— M C————

Banstead, Surrey

(*Daily Telegraph,* September 1978)

So we must be careful and caring. But not all 'older members' take this stance and experience shows that some of the keenest advocates of progress are senior citizens.

Church layout and liturgy are linked; when we come to consider their development we find that the barricades against change are certainly still up, but it is heartening to find PCC members all over the country expressing concern for maintaining a gospel witness relevant to this and the next generation. Beyond that, one hardly dare peer. In one town-centre church, the view was put forward that the parish church might well be the only Christian base in the inner town within five or ten years, so regularly were other churches closing; the speaker urged the PCC to prepare to shoulder the sole burden. They accepted the challenge and undertook a massive development project. Maybe God is calling other churches to assume such a responsibility.

3. THE LANGUAGE OF LITURGY

'It is for the sake of man, not of God, that worship and prayers are required; that man may be made better—that he may be confirmed in a proper sense of his dependent state, and acquire those pious and virtuous dispositions in which his highest improvement consists.'

Hugh Blair

There are many people who, thirty years ago, would have gone to the stake for the 1662 Book of Common Prayer—and the Authorized Version—to judge from their protestations. There are far less now, because familiarity with Alternative Services has brought new debate and understanding of the purpose of liturgy. The new renderings of the Bible have also expanded popular comprehension of the Word.

The English language has undergone a considerable change since World War II. The use of language in the church context parallels this change, though less flamboyantly. In consequence, the BCP is on the way to becoming the preserve of an esoteric appreciation society. If New Series orders are doctrinally sound, who are we to assume outmoded phrases when addressing Almighty God, who is a God of progress and relevance? Who are we to relegate him to the vernacular of a particular date in church history? We shall see later that this argument may also apply to church buildings.

God is giving us new revelations at all levels of life. He monitors scientific and technological progress as he reveals more and more of To-morrow's World. How then do we justify frozen religious expressions, to be repeated generation after generation, often with understanding in inverse proportion to its familiarity?

Always provided that in those parts of the service directly addressed to God (such as the petitions and the praises) we employ the best quality of accurate contemporary English. We may need to perpetuate Cranmer's tautology (for which there was also good reason in the 16c) because of our multi-racial society.

Leading public worship poses special problems, including those imposed by the architecture. We are becoming emancipated from the performer-spectator relationship engendered by Victorian Tractarian ideals. Readings and prayers may be given by others than the parson and, if well done, can be beneficial to the corporate act. There is however one unsuspected hazard: public address or sound reinforcement systems, excellent for improved audibility, may actually accentuate the performer-spectator condition, to the detriment of corporateness. A similar deficiency can be caused when structure interrupts sight-lines.

A problem which is fortunately diminishing is the shortage of meaningful hymns. Anyone accustomed to selecting hymns knows these limitations only too well, even when dipping into You-know-what Praise and the other Sounds . . . A diet of choruses is hardly strong meat, either. But the signs are hopeful.

4. THE MUSIC OF LITURGY

'Some to church repair
Not for the doctrine, but the music there.'
Alexander Pope

Along with good words, we need good music, competently played. The guitar has been a boon in church life in recent years, though somewhat monotonous and requiring amplification in a large building. In contrast, organs have a longer record, require more musical skill, are powerful and need maintenance.

Nineteenth-century organ fever is abating and, apart from the guitar, we are now seeing the return of other instruments into church music. When fully developed this grows into a church orchestra along with the choir. Of course, in the 17th and 18th centuries musicians and singers accompanied the congregation, often from galleries or raised terraces. We are beginning to return to these arrangements and the present trend incorporates organ, piano, string and wind instruments, as well as singers. In family services children will participate with recorders and even yoghourt pots filled with rice. Tambourines are not confined to the Salvation Army. Fortunately there is an increasing number of singable tunes appearing and these encourage congregational response.

Church music ranges from superb musicianship in cathedrals and larger parish churches like Leeds to a handful of more or less lusty enthusiasts in downtown and country areas. Who is to say which is more acceptable to God? It has to be said that sometimes the most touchy and conservative unit in church worship is the choir, or, more particularly, the organist. This is sad, because the leaders in music can bring out wholehearted response by the rest of the congregation in praise and joyful sounds. How many enterprising clergy are frustrated by intractable choirmasters who seem not to realize the brake they are applying to fervour in worship!

There is also the location of the choir. Arranged antiphonally in a chancel, they constitute a separate congregation, especially if they are dressed differently from the remainder. It is clearly an advantage for the choir, organist and organ to be in proximity, but need this be at the front? In pre-Victorian times they were more commonly rearward, whether or not there was a gallery. Wherever they are, may they realize their responsibility to assist and not dominate the rest of the assembly. This is part of the sensitive balance between clergy, people and music.

A recent development is the replacement of choir stalls (mostly Victorian) by well-designed chairs and music fronts, generally disposed in an arc in the chancel and occupied by music groups, of which there may be more than one in a church, operating by rota. If the organ is alongside the chancel and a grand piano is one of the instruments (to say nothing of a trumpet), the singers and musicians, unrobed, can give a splendid lead. With such a chancel arrangement the holy table will doubtless need to be brought forward to a nave dais. This dais can also be used for recitals and drama, and it is worth considering its form.

The shape of a dais projecting into the nave may be rectangular, semi-circular or splayed. Any of these shapes will support the concept of gathering round the table. Usually there will be no more than two steps and if communion rails are desired, these may be removeable; in any case a wide gap in the centre avoids the impression of fencing the table when looking up the centre gangway.

Indeed, we are bound to ask whether a fully-open table area is preferable, with communicants standing to receive the bread and wine. Surely the act of handling the elements is one of fellowship and it has been remarked that seeing the joy on the face of the minister reinforces this mutual delight in the signs and seals of the bread and wine. Such rapport is obviously easier if the recipient is standing.

5. THE GATHERING CHURCH

'The church is the family of God. It is seen in miniature in each family.'
John Ferguson

We began by using the common term *going to church*. The impression is that of a congregation assembling in a purpose-built edifice to make prayers, sing hymns, hear readings and exposition. At the end, we have *been to church*.

To many, this has seemed incomplete. There was inadequate opportunity to fraternise. Standing round the font or near a draughty porch, blocking the exit, discouraged friendly chat and personal ministry. So a few brave vicars suggested coffee after the services. And it caught on. The benefits of lubricated fellowship were soon recognized.

Braver souls went further. They conceived the notion of the Gathered Church. This was variously manifested, but generally included wider activities and koinonia. Implicit in this idea was the bonding together described at the end of Galatians 2. In short, the Family Church was being deliberately planned. Human families were to be set in the context of the church family.

This was the converse of most church programming. Christians had been seen as individuals; soul-winning was aimed at individuals. This remains one valid approach but when outreach is to households as well, new provisions are needed within the church family. These new provisions affect church buildings.

Before we can investigate these new provisions we must analyse the inherited concept of *going to church*. First of all, there is sabbatarianism, the formalised observance of Sunday, fully warranted by Scripture and with undeniable merits. It is not necessary to dwell upon the physical and mental advantages of the First Day when Christianly observed. The dangers of such observance may be less apparent.

Granted that withdrawal from weekday chores (though not for mother?) is beneficial, such recession needs to be positive, as a battery is removed for re-charging. We come out of the daily cycle in order to be strengthened for going back in. The changes of routine is good for us, the divorce from the activity of the other six days is (at least to lay folk) renovating, *provided that* this divorce from daily life does not set up a dichotomy. We are seven-day Christians but the Going to Church syndrome may limit us to a schizo-phrenic religiosity. The factors contributing to such a divided life-style are

1 anachronistic liturgical language emphasizing the divorce from daily life and requiring a finely tuned mental apprehension, and

2 the strange architecture (ancient and/or modern), usually unlike workaday premises.

We will examine these two factors in a moment.

Going to church is also a restrictive term, suggesting mere attendance at an event, rather than active membership of a living body with enormous power at its disposal.

6. AWE IN THE MIND OF THE BELIEVER

'(The) Numinous: the combined feeling of attraction and awe characteristic of man's sense of communion with God and religion.'

Concise Oxford Dictionary

The Church of England grew out of a medieval English Church which promoted the numinous quality of worship. This quality was, of course, more developed in the chancel-bound priesthood. With the introduction of vernacular formats in the mid-16th century some of this awe-fulness rubbed off onto the congregation. The numinous became a wider experi-ence and survived the shock of new liturgy in English instead of Latin. We should not underestimate the tremendous impact of this change in the language of formal worship, even though the native tongue had been used for preaching.

The current change from Prayer Book English to late 20th century English is far less great. If mid-16th century Englishmen discovered the beauty of their own tongue, perhaps we may discover the enhanced range and etymology of that same tongue in our generation. Four hundred years is a long time but with the acceleration in thought and technical innovation during even the last thirty years, it is not surprising that the old Cranmer phrases have an antique ring. Were we considering a period subject (such as Shakespeare's plays) this would present no insuperable problem; but we are handling a subject which ought to be presented in contemporary terms if it is to be relevant. If it isn't we are in a cocoon and the world will equate us with a museum. It was said in an Anglia television programme that 'the church is not in the world to act as a sanctified antiquarian society'.

9

Modern liturgy needs a fine balance between comprehensible traditge is phrases and everyday spoken communication. Inevitably, as languaional never static, fashionable terms and meanings will appear, as they did 400 years ago. Regular revision will therefore be necessary if the numinous is to be retained and our approach to our Father is to remain soul-stirring.

Regardless of whether the script is Cranmer or Alternative Services, a note of awe can be imparted by the reader; and here the cord between the Parsonical Performance and the Hot Line to God is indeed a tightrope. Leadership in church services and meetings constantly needs to portray that God IS Spirit and it is obvious that such perceptive ministry can only derive from the deepest personal walk with the Lord himself.

Just as background music heightens the viewer's mood in television presentations, the music in worship reinforces the impact of the words, to call out an eager response from the congregation. Enthusiasm and awe form a potent combination which can survive Sunday and spill over into the working week, reducing the schizophrenia.

7. AWE IN THE EYE OF THE BEHOLDER

'As it was in the beginning . . .'

The second factor contributing to schizophrenia in churchfolk is the Shrine Syndrome. The so-called Place of Worship becomes an end in itself. There is a permanence in the use and layout of the shrine-church. The monument and its use are accepted as a liturgico-architectural package deal, meddling with which disturbs the tradition. So we must examine this tradition.

We have noted the numinous in liturgy; is there such a thing as the numinous in buildings? Can buildings promote awe? The answer must surely be 'Yes', when we contemplate the greater works of architecture. We need not labour the point. Nor is awe confined to buildings of religious function; Post Office towers are very impressive. But is this the awe we have in mind?

There will be two kinds of awe associated with buildings in use by Christians, constituting a response to 1. the architecture and 2. the deity. If the building is dedicated (to quote the stock legend on foundation stones) 'To the Glory of God', then (1) the architecture will reflect the builders' offering of their craftmanship and (2) there will be a derived awe transmitted to and detected by the sensitive believer. This latter pervasive awe is the gift of God to his people and encourages them to worship and adore him.

It will be noted that we are gazing beyond the mere stones into a realm of greater beauty. The architecture is therefore a sacrament, an outward and visible sign. To over-adore the building may thus approach idolatry, as with excessive regard for any sacrament. The building is a means to an end, even a means of grace, the chief end being the surrender of man to his God.

David Watson, after dealing with eschatological prospects, writes in *I Believe in the Church*:

> 'Thus the church is, or should be, always on the move. Its structures and institutions are at best only temporary, and must always seek to serve the reign of God as it is demonstrated in power in the world.

> 'A church that forgets this will be unwilling or unable to move. It will cling to its forms of worship and patterns of service, its organizations and traditions, as though these were the ultimate end or aim of the church. Such inflexibility will breed stagnation and sterility. The church that will not listen to the voice of God, or will not respond to the promptings of the Spirit (who is ever the Spirit of movement), will be quite unable to speak with relevance or power to the rapidly changing world in which we live.

> 'Flexibility, mobility, sensitivity, fluidity—these are some characteristics of an attitude that results in effective action in God's kingdom. Yet they are difficult, and often we would make structures, traditions, or organization our priority and security. They are valid, but secondary to our availability, our willingness to respond to God according to *his* Spirit, who is often unpredictable and mysterious. The kingdom of God is always dynamic; it cannot be fossilized even for a moment.'

Flexibility is not always a characteristic of church buildings. The grid system of pews is a major factor in this, closely followed by the legacy of Victorian chancel layout. Therefore services are strait-jacketted and wider uses are hindered.

Mobility applies to people and increases with flexibility in furniture and buildings. If the floor is cluttered, movement is restricted. This may prevent after-service fellowship and experimental ordering.

Sensitivity is needed in experimentation, whether liturgical or extended usage; it is also needed in architectural alterations, taking care not to prejudice future developments as well as maintaining an appropriate quality. New work will be plainly modern in design but sympathetic to the older context; mere copyism is not called for, lest we fall into the trap of relating God to a past architectural vernacular. We saw how this also applied to language. Sensitivity is certainly essential when introducing new wine into old skins.

Fluidity is not confined to wine or leaking roofs. The flow or circulation of people through buildings is critical to effective use. It is always worth considering a progression from street to sanctuary and thus we return to our notion of the numinous in buildings. Most churches are consecrated; does this imply super-dedication? And anyway, can inanimate objects be consecrated, other than being merely set apart or dedicated? Perhaps consecration ought to be limited to Christians . . . A warning might be that the sanctuary is not more holy than the street but offers a space more congenial for a specific purpose or action. Holiness reposes in people, not places; in souls, not sites.

It seems we are needing centres for training people to live—and to die.

8. THE ALL-IN CHURCH

A gaggle of geese
A pride of lions
A gathering of Christians

In many parishes, especially inner urban, there are people in bed-sits, hostels and tower blocks. They need companionship and mental stimulation. For them, Sunday can be the loneliest day of the week.

It is unlikely that such people will find deep satisfaction in 'going to church' for services. They, like others, will welcome a more prolonged 'gathering' with a wider range of activity than liturgical exercise; Acts 14.27 '. . . when they arrived, they *gathered* the church together and declared all that God had done with them.' Surely this was more than a sermon?

The Americans have already developed this extended assembly, which may yet supersede our traditional short morning and evening Sunday services. In 1977 the Archbishop of York was deploring what he called the 'cafeteria system' of church services and suggesting that there should be one Sunday service for everyone. One gathering a Sunday would certainly maintain one congregation though creche minders and some other regular leaders might need a rota; shift workers also present a problem.

In Acts 12.12 '. . . many were *gathered* together and were praying' so let us assume that it is desirable to have the total church family together at one time each Sunday. With a large congregation, this may strain the accommodation, whether the time is morning or evening, and no standard pattern can be laid down. The issue being pleaded is that of the Family Church, meeting and working corporately rather than a brief encounter of individuals. The *Derby Diocesan News* suggested that 'One well-attended, well-planned meeting for worship, learning and fellowship, with all members of the local Christian community present would be more inspiring, more effective, and more in keeping with apostolic practice than our present division into morning and evening congregations.' It also claimed that the proliferation of Sunday services made people surprisingly selfish: 'I must have my eight o'clock service' was a comment often heard.

Of many permutations, one possible timetable might be:

11.00	Reception: coffee, notices, news, personal exchanges, bookstall, fixing meetings and appointments . . .
11.30	Liturgical service and classes, with a theme for the day; creche.
12.30	Fruit juice; togetherness.
1.00	Lunch: buffet, formal or picnic.
1.30	Informal meeting or groups; discussion; counselling; confirmation instruction; games; music. The annual or special parochial meeting.
2.30	Disperse.

This kind of programme could be adapted to run in a similar way from teatime onwards. The point being pleaded is for extended, comprehensive gathering, even though not everyone will be present all the time. Such arrangements may commence in a small way monthly and will, to some extent, be conditioned by the premises.

Those churches with Parish Education, or where young people leave the service after 15 minutes, should find enough flexibility to retain their procedures (unless the ancillary accommodation is in a hall or school some distance away so that children have to be taken and picked up). The important issue is the principle of *gathering* as opposed to *going to church*.

Similarly, Saturday can be the loneliest night of the week. Open house in a church lounge complex from 6 to 10 p.m. can meet a widespread need; not everyone wants to spend Saturday evening at a pub or a cinema, or even before the mini-screen. No great organization is required for an all-age club evening where whole families as well as the unattached can drop in and eat, chat, play draughts, table tennis or Monopoly, even sing and dance. There is no need for an epilogue or direct evangelism, though during the evening there might be a 'spot' with a short film, a talk or an organized game for those who want it, leaving the rest to enjoy their preference in other parts of the building. Non-Christian friends can be introduced this way, and can be shown something of the church's care.

Which brings us to accommodation. Obviously, the wider the range of activities the more facilities are required; certainly a central lounge with catering provision will be needed, as well as small group rooms and games spaces. The old duo of Church and Church Hall is unlikely to suffice.

There are certain well-defined elements in this family church concept; for example: the Ministry of Food. Eating together does great things for the fellowship. Fears that a few ladies will have to work hard and long in a church kitchen are not fulfilled when the kitchen is properly designed and equipped. At present the image of parochial kitchens is awful and there is sometimes a defeatist attitude over catering. Yet experience shows that rarely is a church without at least one lady who is happy to assume overall responsibility for this department. She need not be a culinary *prima donna*. Husbands are, of course, expert at washing up and if the lady in charge recruits a few friends to share the preparation, there is developed an important ministry in the church. And not only on Sunday and Saturday, but a mid-week light lunch for mothers and children, senior citizens, businessmen and others who are around. Always, food will be properly charged and paid for, except in cases of hardship.

One of the advantages of the all-Family gathering is that different age-groups mix, to their mutual benefit; over-40s can still beat teenagers at table tennis and parents can play with other people's children (this can be most revealing).

Having said all this, are we to promote a mere social club? The answer will depend on declared policy thrashed out in the PCC meetings. Christianity is becoming a fringe ethos in Britain (how many school leavers can say the

Lord's Prayer?). We can no longer assume that our neighbours realize that Christians are ordinary sinners who have been inwardly transformed supernaturally. Perhaps we do not demonstrate this outwardly, for one reason or another. We would like to invite them to our church but maybe reception facilities are limited; perhaps the services are strong meat, or sparse, or dull . . .

Therefore we need pre-evangelism, a half-way house, where those unfamiliar with Christian goings-on may be reassured and, perhaps to their surprise, discover that believers are actually human and not a bunch of esoteric nuts.

One vicar has said: 'When non-Christians come to ask me to baptize their baby and I require them to participate in church life for a period, what can I offer them—and where?'

This is not merely to consider suitable premises. It is primarily a human need and the response must be planned in terms of human relationships in the sight of God, although as yet God may be unknown to some of the potential participants. The spatial accommodation will follow when the activities have been proposed. Buildings must serve people and not *vice versa*.

This is a far cry from the social notion; it is also a far cry from the way most churches use their premises, though it must be added that few churches possess plant which lends itself to such a life-style. If a church is to be a caring community, especially for its own members, it needs to foster deep friendships, wrought in its week by week life and forged within the tensions of present-day society. The growing concept of House Groups (not mere bible-study groups but deeper and more inter-committed) is showing a way of such forging. Thus, whenever and wherever the church gathers, it grows; and growth is surely the *sine qua non* of a healthy church family. Growth will be theological (i.e. with wider apprehension) as well as numerical. So we must look out of the windows . . .

9. THE ALL-OUT CHURCH

Activity will derive from what the Church regards as its function; what is the Church in business for?

There used to be jokes about parsons working one day a week. Nobody ever joked about church buildings only working one day a week; or even a few hours a week. Perhaps it's not funny; and anyway, how can you use a church from Monday to Saturday?

Concern must be aroused over the *non-use* as much as the actual use of our parish churches. Non-use spells stagnation, and stagnation leads to decay. Whether you occupy a building or not, the roofs wear out, the gutters choke and the paint flakes. A building which suffers sharp temperature gradients due to intermittent heating and bad ventilation will induce condensation, which is the enemy of organs, metalwork and decoration.

A building that is under-used is under-familiar. Entering it, therefore, requires an effort of will. Consequently, a population culturally estranged from churchgoing gives it a miss and on the whole views the Christian denominations as closed in-sects and anachronistic drop-outs. This is beyond mere apathy or alienation and it culminates in a phobia about entering a church for a service, with its non-telly vocabulary, its extraordinary garmentation and the often dispersed congregation. In some circles, to attend a Sunday service would be the quickest way to incur the ribaldry of family and friends. Going religious is still unfashionable.

Christians, nevertheless, are charged with the responsibility of making more Christians. This process can be accomplished anywhere but sooner or later there will be the welcome into the gathered fellowship—in a church building. If we are concerned only to perpetuate historic procedures, new arrivals will have to learn the technical talk, the postural responses and the decorous behaviour.

But if we are concerned to apply the Christian Gospel to life in the launderette we may find our churches something of a liability. Rarely do people convert from a man-centred stance to a Christ-centred ethos in a moment. There is a process, more or less gradual, which needs encouragement; it needs a halfway house. Most churches in their procedures and premises demand a fullway commitment.

Why then, do we neglect to deploy our churches to suit this wider need, the need to encourage newcomers as well as to permit enterprising activities within the church family? It seems we are often bound by traditions which we have never questioned.

False assumptions about the building. Subconsciously we relate churches to shrines or even mausoleums. We tolerate the Old Testament concept of the Holy Place, unrelated to work, or leisure or education, only viable for Worship—and Sunday worship at that. The Victorian emphasis upon the monumental and the formal has left us with an attitude to churches which sees any use but liturgical worship as incongruous. Very often, the sheer size of the building reinforces this disability.

False assumptions about the Church. The true Church is, of course, people; more or less healthy, active, involved humanity. Is it to leave the fun, the fears and the frustrations in the porch like wet umbrellas when it gathers to practise its calling as the People of God? So often, it seems embarrassing to laugh in church; someone might frown. Non-fun quenches the joy one ought to experience in singing psalms and hymns. Is that why there are so few radiant countenances?

False assumptions about the Almighty. It is a fair guess that most people hold God in their mind's eye (to fall back on privately in moments of crisis), whether they openly acknowledge his existence or not. Church buildings invite recollection of Him, which is expressed as reverence. Leaving aside the effect of doctrine upon our reactions, the conclusion dawns upon us that God is here, that He is localised in this building and probably in one part more than another, and even in one piece of furniture. So we speak of the House of God; and we are wrong because there is nothing in the Bible to support this syndrome. The church building is the house of the *People of God,* which upholds the New Testament notion of the Church as a corpus.

This brings us back to the seven-day week, for the human corpus does not stop breathing six days out of seven and become Seventh-Day Inhalers.

Apart from our attitudes and our assumptions, what else keeps churches under-used? Many things, but principally: regiments of pews standing to attention, limiting free assembly; unsuitable heating; tiresome acoustics. Small numbers in a large building become de-scaled. So we may need to adapt and re-order. We should expect to see buildings serving people. Let's wear out our churches by use rather than non-use.

10. MOTIVES FOR CHANGE

'If the Church is one Family, the Church buildings are our Family Home. We need to lose the concept of "going to church", with the congregation simply coming straight into the church building, and then out again with no real meeting. It is rather a matter of "being the Church"; each one of us is a vital member of the Body of Christ— belonging, sharing, caring, meeting, talking, being together. This all needs the right sort of Family Home for its expression.'

Brian Morley

We have seen the dangers of freezing liturgy and ossifying the use and layout of church premises. How nice (we may feel) if our buildings were less bleak, more flexible in use.

In some parts of the world, a copy of even the meanest English church would surpass the standard of surrounding native shacks. Does this mean we should deliberately restrict the architectural standard of our assembly point in Britain? Or may we call for higher quality multi-functional centres?

The answer lies in the Church's calling to make disciples. The local church is always set in a particular cultural environment. This may be East, West or Third World. Its reach-out will need to be intelligible to the natives and in terms of their familiar culture.

People find it difficult to leave their herd, whether they be natives of Bangkok, Brighton or Baltimore, and this is entirely reasonable. It means, however, that our spoken and demonstrated witness to Christ (our life-style) will proclaim our understanding of, and (dare we say it?) superiority over, the culture in which we are set. While we are being all things to all men for the sake of the Gospel, we will be showing the superior way.

Does this suggest that the superior way of Jesus will require correspondingly superior places of Christian assembly? To this, no standard answer is possible. Moreover, a church fellowship which embarks upon building development for its own comfort will find little true satisfaction or profit. The motive behind a development scheme, however modest or however comprehensive must be to reinforce the twin apogees of parish policy already mentioned:

1. To strengthen those already within the fellowship, and

2. To bring others in,

through Jesus Christ.

Try standing outside a church (?your church) and asking yourself: Suppose I had no experience of church life, could I be persuaded to enter that building? Do the solid storm-doors warn: 'No Entry'. Does the building speak of Success or Failure? because the world is conditioned to think of the Church in terms of shrinkage and failure.

You may answer that God does not look for success or failure, only faithfulness. But the world does. Business life, TV advertising and social assessment are geared to success or failure. We must accept this as a fact of contemporary life. If our churches, often set amid prolific memorials to the dead, speak of decay and failure, we will find our image (don't let us despise contemporary terms) and our witness impaired.

The trend in politics, commerce and social life is for openness, accessibility community. Prison-like entrances run counter to this; we need to let the public see into our buildings, to astonish folk by revealing Christians actually laughing and enjoying themselves in clean, well-appointed surroundings. This is how we will attract the other patrons of the launderette.

If we can grasp a renewed vision of total Christianity with emphasis on Gathering and Going we shall require premises with the utmost flexibility in order to respond to developing opportunities.

Only those churches which are on the march, and who find their premises a hindrance, will consider a building project. The rest will quietly soldier on until demobilization.

11. MOTIVES FOR NO-CHANGE

'For the average Christian the Church is just there. People don't expect a divine service to be suddenly withdrawn as if it were an unprofitable railway line.'

Prof. David Martin

The on-going repetition of historic forms of church worship and routine imparts a sense of continuity, even permanence, into an otherwise shifting, changing impermanent world. Such impermanence has now even assailed Christian marriage. Why then add to the instability of society by changing familiar church procedures?

This argument implies a near-perfection in the ways of the past (be they liturgy, pastoral methods or architecture) which can only be marred by change. It also betrays a resistance to change, which commands a measure of sympathy.

Can we therefore conscientiously recommend change in church life and buildings? The answer is historical and simply that, whether we have realised it or not, church life *has* changed and by its very nature as leaven in the world it must inevitably interact with its lump. And the lump has certainly changed; family life, shopping, work, education, differ enormously from thirty years ago. If we do not modify our call, we speak to a generation which no longer exists.

The sheet-anchor permanence we desire must surely repose in the Gospel doctrines, leaving the Church free to interpret these theologically to each succeeding generation in terms which are relevant to local culture and insights. Inevitably this will modify the way in which the Church goes about its calling.

It may be protested that the Church's calling is independent of buildings, so why bother to maintain them, much less up-date them? We cannot, however, ignore their existence and it is difficult to believe that it would be practicable to abandon them in favour of other places of assembly, such as private houses. Therefore we must make the best of them, which calls for wide pragmatism. Christianity appeals to simple folk as well as the intellectual, so the treatment of church premises will need to reflect all levels of local culture.

At this point we are brought up against R. J. Sider's arguments in *Rich Christians in an Age of Hunger,* where the worldly lifestyle of Western Christians gets a rough handling. It must be agreed that there is certainly no justification for embellishing new church lounges and meeting spaces with finishes and accessories which are neither functional nor durable. Nevertheless, each church has the duty to determine its policy within a prayer-based study of its needs.

No doubt we all accept that Christians must contribute to the alleviation of starvation; this need not be at the expense of other Christian obligations, such as the expansion of the Kingdom of God in Britain. For instance: is the curate's stipend a priority? do not dilapidated buildings prejudice evangelism, without which there will be no effective church in the future?

When the woman at Bethany poured the alabastar jar of expensive perfume over Christ and the religious people complained that the poor were being deprived through such apparant extravagance, Jesus commended her action on the grounds that she had given the best to him, trusting him to make available consequential benefits to more people than she could ever help. The same principle applied in the feeding of the five thousand.

Could it be that our support of relief charities needs to be balanced by the complementary strengthening of our home base so that more people will be drawn to contribute? Maybe, as Ronald Sider suggests, this will demand a simpler personal lifestyle for Christians, and no realistic Christian will argue against that. But the corporate body of Christians also needs to work out a lifestyle which is to the point and also involves premises which are equally attractive. We may not have alabastar jars of perfume but it must surely be pleasing to the Lord when a church council resolves to pour out a quality offering to honour him and in faith that he will multiply the results of the enterprise.

But let us turn to resistances to change in the church premises. In Britain, when building work is proposed which will enlarge or improve church facilities, the point is always raised (as we have said)that the money would be better employed alleviating distant hunger; and this is very emotive.

Upon examination, this issue is not always found to be so clear-cut; and this is where we come back to culture, of which buildings are a part, or even a symbol.

The simple shelter may be entirely appropriate in simple communities around the world. In such an environment, anything pretentious would surely be a hindrance to witness. In more affluent cultures, however, the cheap building may be regarded by the natives as failure. Let us have simplicity by all means, but with *quality*. Where to draw the line can only be determined after prayer and study. It is, however, an interesting fact that members of church committees who deplore spending money on improving premises on the grounds that overseas needs are paramount, are often those with the finest homes; to suggest that they should sell their car(s) or refrigerator to bring their personal lifestyle down to their overseas counterparts is to invite a rebuff.

We will communicate within our own culture. Britain certainly has not a predominantly Christian culture and a few more African missionaries would be welcome here. If they came, would we expect them to live in the style of rural Africa, which is our impression of what is called 'the mission field'? Moreover, if the native church in Britain is not strong, how can it help to support those overseas counterparts for whom our objectors are so solicitous?

It is true that God can, and does, work outside church buildings. But sooner or later the newcomer will be brought to meet the membership in a church building; if there are double standards, who will be let down?

So who finds the money to pay for the accommodation required by a Gathering Church? This question separates the mean from the joyous, because one of the most rewarding aspects of a building project is the giving; this searches out a person's commitment to the Lord; it tests faith and provides occasions for teaching. The very display of improving a church can be made the opportunity for witness to the neighbourhood. Success!

12. THE WHEELS IN MOTION

It is not possible to discuss buildings apart from the activity they enclose.

Those architects engaged in providing for the extended use of church plant find their challenges coming from the livelier parishes; experience shows that the happiest results come when a disciplined routine is followed.

If buildings are to serve people, a deep study is necessary of the pastoral, liturgical, educational and missionary aspects of the church. This will call for a small working party to plumb these aspects with a perceptive architect.

When the current situation has been accurately appraised and the needs and opportunities assessed of a time-scale, which may stretch some years ahead, the architect will be able to suggest the options for building alterations, extensions or new premises. This may be a phased development but always it must be a master plan to avoid inhibiting future progress.

In due course, the working party will take their proposals to the PCC, the architect being their spokesman. If the PCC is minded to proceed, there are diocesan and civil approaches to be made. It is then desirable to share the project with the parochial constituency at a special church meeting. This meeting will fall into three parts, plus refreshments:

1. The vicar will outline the present state of church life, its needs, restrictions, opportunities; he will draw upon the working party's findings and mention policy for the future, and how this will demand altered accommodation.

2. The architect, using an overhead projector or other aids, will describe the solution to the needs, in terms of buildings. He will mention costs and answer questions.

3. The treasurer will explain the financing of the project and introduce a take-away brochure, inviting people to subscribe in one form or another.

It is undoubtedly startling to some church members if a scheme costing many thousands of pounds is put forward and they are told that the PCC proposes to implement it at the congregation's expense. This is probably the crudest way of launching a project and, however obvious and praise-worthy a scheme, the finances deserve good public relations treatment; otherwise, money becomes a barrier from the start, instead of one of the most exciting and deeply spiritual aspects of the whole enterprise.

A more encouraging way of presenting the financial challenge to the congregation is for the PCC to demonstrate its own response; when the aggregate pledge of its members is announced at the general meeting, a lead is given.

We should remember that few church members have been involved in a building project; some have never even met an architect. They are therefore naturally apprehensive. How are they to know that God, who is a rich Father, intends to honour their commitment? They have no precedent at this level.

Money does not grow on trees but pennies *do* come from heaven—and so do pounds—as many PCCs have discovered, often to their astonishment. With proper homework and prayer before venturing to push on available doors, God has opened the way with financial blessing. It seems that this generally occurs on projects where emphasis is placed on direct giving, possibly aided by diocesan sources and Christian trusts.

Surely, is not inflation here to stay? We therefore must expect inflation on building costs, and this is difficult to forecast. It might seem therefore, that before money collected can be turned into buildings, there will be a wastage due to inflation. This is only partly true because (i) money received is normally placed on deposit, thereby earning interest, and (ii) treasurers report that individual giving increases to keep pace with inflation.

Architects are used to being told 'Of course, we are a poor parish', yet we all have a heavenly cheque book and there are many dramatic instances of drawing on God's account in funding development projects.

In Luke 6.30 Jesus says 'the measure you give will be the measure you get back'. No doubt this includes money as well as love and other transferable commodities. Is it not Scriptural to give *in order* to get back? Should we not *invest,* expecting a return? This can apply to individuals as well as the Church body, for it is not uncommon to hear people say when new accommodation is opened: 'I thought I was giving sacrificially, but I am better off now than when we started'. This is surely God's way of measuring.

13. THE HOLINESS OF BEAUTY

'Beauty is intrinsically edifying; gossip, daydreaming and mere self-expression, intrinsically unedifying.'

Aldous Huxley

In some Christian circles art is considered an expensive luxury and a worldly extravagance. As Saki wrote: 'I always say beauty is only sin deep'. Of course, art and beauty are not always synonymous but many of us are custodians of beautiful buildings. Beauty is subjective and, as Sir Hugh Casson put it: 'The British love permanence more than they love beauty'. Most church buildings (at least, those over thirty years old) are permanent; it could be that we mistake this for beauty, just as we confuse tradition with truth. But beauty, like truth, is not confined to the past. It need not be destroyed by later accretions. It may, in fact, be enhanced.

During the last thirty years there has been a change in the use, the furnishing and the equipment of all types of building. Offices are planned differently and are better equipped; carpets are found in schools, in domestic bathrooms and in shops. Lighting and heating are more developed. Austerity may remain a virtue, but it is no longer attractive. People now expect an environment with a more human scale and greater amenity and flexibility.

If the church is to hold its own at this level, compared with, say, well-appointed modern pubs, it has to *appeal* to people. We know we have the Word of Life—but folk outside don't. The miracle is that so many people are converted today, in spite of us and our premises. How many more wait to be attracted?

> Give grace to us, our families and friends,
> and to all our neighbours in Christ;
> that we may serve him in one another,
> and love as he loves us.

APPENDIX

Re-tooling Church Plant
(which does not imply destroying beauty)

Remodelling of churches falls into three categories:

A Liturgical re-ordering
This is usually confined to furniture and incorporates a more central working area on a dais. The holy table will be brought forward, reading desks will face the congregation, choir stalls may be replaced by chairs and music stands. Preaching may be from a lectern. Communion rails are often portable and may be benches which can also serve as seating at other times. Some pews are generally removed, maybe with consequent levelling of the floor.

B Enclosure of space(s) within the church
The west end or side aisles receive folding or fixed partitions to provide lounges, meeting rooms, catering, lavatories. Liturgical re-ordering often accompanies such alterations.

C Extension of church to provide Meeting Spaces
This may be combined with **A** and **B** above.
Extensions are usually attached physically to the church and may be single or two-storey, possibly incorporating a flat.

In **B** and **C** it is important to introduce people into a main Lounge area as soon as possible on entering, in order to encourage a relaxed demeanour and to provide an opportunity for friendly exchanges. Even to stand on a pile carpet inculcates a feeling of well-being. Such lounges are invaluable at the conclusion of services or at intervals in synods, recitals, dramatic presentations or other functions for which re-ordered churches can be so suitable an auditorium. The extent of other compartments and refreshment facilities will be a matter for local determination. There are no standard solutions; every scheme must be tailor-made.

The various diagrams on page 24 and on the inside front and back covers illustrate some sample solutions to the problems of liturgical reordering set by traditional church buildings.

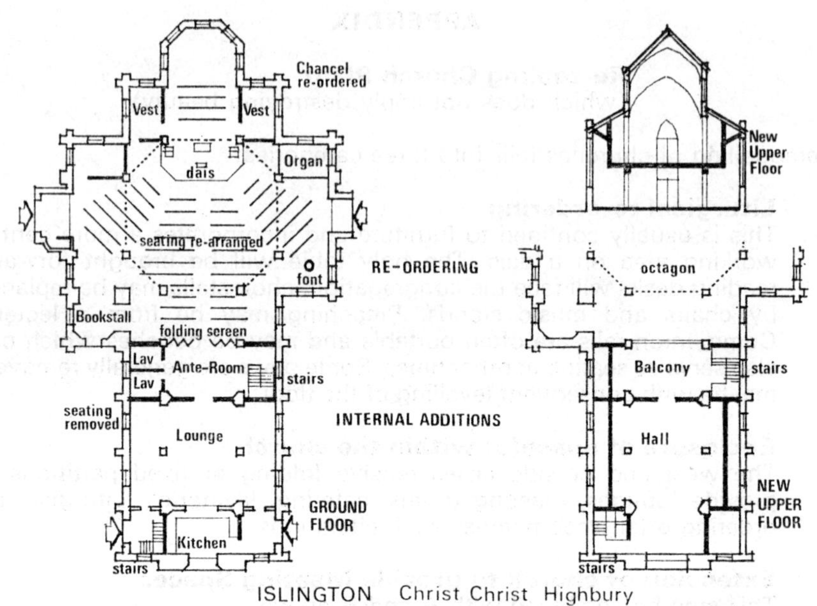
Chancel
re-ordered
Vest
Vest
Organ
dais
seating re-arranged
RE-ORDERING
font
Bookstall
folding screen
Lav
Ante-Room
stairs
Lav
seating
removed
Lounge
INTERNAL ADDITIONS
GROUND
FLOOR
Kitchen
stairs
ISLINGTON   Christ Christ Highbury
New
Upper
Floor
octagon
Balcony
stairs
Hall
NEW
UPPER
FLOOR
stairs
Vestries
organ
choir
organ
N Aisle
Nave
S Aisle
BEFORE
5
6
7
8
Meeting
space
screen
choir
RE-ORDERING
Vestry
INTERNAL
ADDITIONS
Admin
dais
seating facing
dais
Vestry
4
Porch
folding screen
Foyer
Kitchen
Lounge
ceiling over
Lav
folding screen
3
1
ceiling
2
Meeting
N E S W
AFTER
SURBITON   Christ Church